LASTING IMPRESSIONS

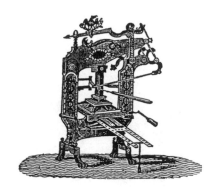

LASTING IMPRESSIONS

A Short History
of English Publishing in
Quebec

Bruce Whiteman

An AEAQ Edition

Véhicule Press

Montréal

AN AEAQ EDITION

Published with the assistance of the Quebec Minister of
Culture and Communications, and The Canada Council.

The publisher would like to extend special thanks to the
Department of Rare Books and Special Collections of the
McGill University Libraries, and to Paul Davies for ongoing
inspiration.

Cover photo: John Lovell (1865) courtesy of the Notman
Archives of the McCord Museum of Canadian History.
Cover design: Mark Garland
Design and imaging: Simon Garamond.
Printing: Imprimerie d'Édition Marquis Ltée.

CANADIAN CATALOGUING IN PUBLICATION DATA

Whiteman, Bruce, 1952-
   Lasting impressions : a short history of English
publishing in Quebec

"An AEAQ Edition".
Includes index.
ISBN 1-55065-051-3

1. Publishers and publishing—Quebec (Province).
I. Association des éditeurs anglophones du Québec.
II. Title.

Z488.3.Q8W44 1994   070.5'09714   C94-900136-8

Véhicule Press, P.O.B. 125 Place du Parc Station, Montreal,
Quebec H2W 2M9. Distributed by General Distribution
Services, 30 Lesmill Road, Don Mills, Ontario M3B 2T6

Printed in Canada on acid-free paper.

CONTENTS

For my friends in the trade

PREFACE

As the curator of a large rare book collection with extensive holdings of European and Canadian books, I work surrounded by the products of half a millenium of printing and publishing. For a scholar interested in the history of the book it can be fascinating; for a poet it is a sobering day-job. Publishers form a kind of sub-class of culture heroes, or some of them do at least, to whom the social scientists have yet to turn their attention. Writers know something of this, for all that they are given to complaining about "their" publishers. Readers, too, when they stop to think, have much to be grateful for to the men and women who have, at least in the modern sense, made reading possible. Gutenberg was the first publisher to go bankrupt, but hardly the last.

English publishing in Quebec has taken place in un-usual circumstances, and this modest book is an at-tempt to highlight some of its successes and to view them within a lightly drawn cultural context. It is not a scholarly book, although I have made every attempt to be as accurate as possible, and the results of original research might be spotted here and there. At the same time, I have drawn on a wide variety of printed sources to piece together this history, and here express my gratitude to the many writers and scholars who have written about the history of printing and publishing in Canada, especially Quebec. Added to that largely unsung group must be the even more obscure work of the librarians and private collectors — mostly, in my case, associated with McGill — who worked with booksellers and auctioneers over the course of a century and a half to put together the comprehensive book and manuscript collection without which a book like this could not have been contemplated, much less written.

A number of friends and colleagues read and commented on parts or all of this book when it was a manuscript in progress, and I am conscious of my debts to them: Warren Baker, Michel Brisebois, Douglas Fetherling, Patricia Fleming, Ken Norris, Nellie Reiss, Carl Spadoni, and Richard Virr. Simon Dardick, the Quebec publisher who agreed to publish the book, was helpful and supremely objective at all stages. As always, members of the staff of the Department of Rare Books and Special Collections at McGill were helpful and understanding. The illustrations, mostly taken from copies of books in the McGill collections, are used courtesy of the McGill University Libraries. Pat Kennedy of the National Archives of Canada kindly arranged for the photograph from the Neilson Papers. The photograph of John Lovell was provided by the Notman Photographic Archives of the McCord Museum of Canadian History.

This book began life as a project of the AEAQ, the English-language publishers association of Quebec, and I here express my appreciation to Endre Farkas, then chair, for asking me to undertake it.

Bruce Whiteman
Montreal
January 27, 1994

LASTING IMPRESSIONS

A Short History
of English Publishing in
Quebec

The invention of printing with moveable type in the mid-fifteenth century has been of enormous and far-reaching importance. It is one of the few human achievements without which Western civilization as we know it would be unrecognizably different. "Out of a full heart of reverence, then, it is most fitting to embalm the memory of Gutenberg," rhapsodizes the author of *Gutenberg, or the World's Benefactor*, a nineteenth-century book for boys on the art of printing. Gutenberg's ability to synthesize traditional technology, such as the wine press, with his invention of casting individual identical

1 5

letters from metal has indeed profoundly affected the course of history and private life ever since.

From Mainz in Germany, where the two-volume 42-line Bible appeared around 1455, printing spread with remarkable speed. In less than fifty years there were *officinae* (print shops) in hundreds of European towns and cities, and by the end of the century almost 30,000 editions of books had been published. The first book published in the New World was printed in Mexico in 1539 — the *Breve y más compendioso Doctrina Christiana en lengua Mexicana y Castellana* issued by Juan Pablos in Mexico City — and within a century printing had spread to both South America (1584) and the continental United States (1640). It was not, of course, by accident that the first European printed book was the Bible, and it is noteworthy that the products of many of the first presses were liturgical, theological, or biblical. Though much of the earliest printing in Canada was to consist of government documents, religious printing would also be a staple well into the nineteenth century.

All the more surprising it is, then, that no printing press was brought to New France. In France itself the press was very closely controlled by the authorities until the time of the Revolution. A system of privileges and government censorship meant that any controversial work was usually published beyond French borders — normally in Switzerland or Holland — and then smuggled into France. Alternatively a book might be printed in Paris or Rouen but given a fictitious or borrowed imprint; such was the case, for example, with Rousseau's *Émile*, which purported to be published in Amsterdam but was in fact printed and issued in Paris. Given these circumstances it is not surprising that there was often a member of the book trade in the Bastille. The writer and minor philosophe Jacques-Pierre Brissot de Warville, for example, passed two months of *embastillement* in 1784 for distributing forbidden printed material.

The ecclesiastical as well as the civil authorities took a deep interest in the control of what was printed and read, and the first papal *Index* of books prohibited to Catholic readers appeared in 1559, only one century after the invention of printing. Bishop Laval and his five successors in New France did much to ensure that the colonists read only what was approved. The records document more than one request for a printing press to be sent to New France, but these requests were ignored. It was once thought that Pontbriand, who was Bishop

This entry from the records of Brown and Gilmore, the first printers in Quebec, describes the terms of their partnership and itemizes certain disbursements. It is dated August 5, 1763.
National Archives of Canada, Neilson Papers,
MG 24-B1, Vol. 49, p. 2.

of Quebec at the time of the Conquest, had his own private press, but the two printed *mandements* dated 1759 which support this theory have been shown to be later fabrications.

The earliest press to be set up in what is now Canada was brought by Bartholomew Green to Halifax in 1751. But it was not until after the Treaty of Paris in 1763, which brought the Seven Years War to an end and saw control of New France pass officially from France to Great Britain, that a printer came to Quebec. William Brown (1737-89) and his partner Thomas Gilmore (1741?-73) went to Quebec City from Philadelphia in 1764. Like all the early Canadian printers they were necessarily publishers, pressmen, editors, and salesmen all in one. A book trade as such did not develop in Quebec until the nineteenth century, and no publisher could make ends meet by publishing only books. Publishing was largely by commission rather than "on spec," and most printer-publishers made their living by issuing a newspaper and doing job printing. As late as 1831, a guidebook to Quebec City noted that its three printers "are employed chiefly for the public business, hand bills, and upon newspapers." Brown and Gilmore set the pattern by starting the bilingual *Quebec Gazette/La Gazette de Québec*. The first issue of this, the first Quebec news-paper, appeared from their shop on rue St-Louis on June 21, 1764. "As every kind of knowledge is not only entertaining and instructive to individuals," they wrote in "The Printers to the Publick" in the inaugural issue,

> but a benefit to the community, there is great reason to hope, that a NEWS-PAPER, properly conducted, and written with Accuracy, Freedom, and Impartiality, cannot fail of meeting with universal encouragement; especially as it is allowed by all, that such a paper is at present much wanted in this colony.

If Gutenberg could have been made to rise from the dead and transported to the shop of Brown and Gilmore, he would have found nothing unfamiliar. The craft of printing had changed scarcely at all in 300 years. All type was composed by hand and copies were printed one sheet at a time on a wooden press. Press, type, and paper were all imported from outside the colony, as indeed were books in large numbers.

The *Quebec Gazette* and Brown and Gilmore's pay to do some government printing permitted them to

TO THE CITIZENS

OF THE TOWN AND DISTRICT OF MONTREAL.

GENTLEMEN,

THE ESTABLISHEMENT of a PERIODICAL PAPER, appears to me as to many others a project of such nature as to deserve your attention in every respects, by which means trade and Commerce will be carried on with a greater facility, correspondance with a greater ease, and a noble emulation will naturaly ensue to the great advantage of the publick, the Citizen will with more speed and in a concifer manner communicate his ideas : hence the progress of Arts and Sciences in general, and the necessary introduction to concord, and union amongst individuals, from which flows several advantages to Society, which you are more sensible of than I can express, and to long to be here enumerated.

These advantages are not less with respect to private interest, the facility of giving notice to the publick at any time of the sale of Goods or Merchandises, Moovables, Houses, Lands, besides the conveniency of advertising for loft effects, Slaves deferted from their Masters, the want of Clarks, or of Servants, and many other things that the opportunity of this paper will offer.

I propose to fill a Sheet with Publick Advertisements and other affairs, immediately concerning trade and Commerce ; to which will be added, some diversified Pieces of Litterature. I dare flatter myself, as I hope, Gentlemen, you will encourage this, my feeble Beginning, that you will in a short time fee with satisfaction not only a great variety of Notices, and Advertisements, but also a Collection of facts both entertaining and instructive. I will endeavour to procure a choice Collection of the Neweft Pieces ; and I dont doubt but this will ftir up the genius of many who have remain'd in a state of inaction, or could not communicate their Productions without the help of the Press.

I will insert in the above Paper or Gazette every thing that one or more Gentlemen will be pleafed to communicate to me, provided always no mention be made of Religion, Government or News concerning the present affairs, unless I was anthoris'd from Government for fo Doing; my intention being only to confine myself in what concerns Advertisements, Commercial and Litterary affairs.

If the Title of Board of Intelligence or Commercial and Litterary Gazette, which I propose to give this Periodical Paper, be not found convenient, I will be glad to receive any Gentlemen's advice on the subject, as also any objections which might be made against the following Conditions.

CONDITIONS.

THE Subfcription money will be two and a half Spanish Dollars per Annum.

THE Subscribers will pay one Spanish Dollar for every Advertifement inferted in the faid Papers, during three Weeks fuccessively.

THOSE that are not Subfcribers will pay one and a half Spanish Dollar for every Advertifement printed thrice as above.

Every one that is not a Subfcriber may have the Paper at 10 Coppers.

THE faid Paper will be printed in a quarto Sheet of Paper, and will be delivered every Wednesday, to begin in Jun 3th. 1778.

All Perfons who chufes to Subfcribe are defired to let me know their Name, and their place of abode.

I have the honour to be, with a fincere defire, to contribute as much as is in my power to the advantage, and publick fatisfaction.

GENTLEMEN,

Your moft Obedient,
and Humble Servant,
F. MESPLET, Printer.

Fleury Mesplet's prospectus of 1778 soliciting subscriptions for the *Gazette du commerce et littéraire*. The prospectus was bilingual, with the French version on the verso.

1788.   NUM. XXIII.

THE *Hmillfveeny*

MONTREAL GAZETE
GAZETTE. DE MONTREAL.

THURSDAY, June 5.   JEUDI, 5 Juin.

CONSTANTINOPLE, *December* 29.

THE Grand Seignior has declared the Captain Pacha Grand Admiral of the Black Sea, and Generalissimo of the troops in that part of the Ottoman domains. This honor and distinction is no less due to his merit, than to the sum of money which he brought from Egypt to the public treasury, and which is said to amount to fifty millions of dollars, besides six millions, which he sent before. His first enterprize, it is said, will be a decent on the Crimea, next spring, with a corps of 25,000 picked men, to endeavor the capture of that peninsula from the Russians.

LONDON, *February* 1.

The Field Mareschal Laudon will certainly command an army against the Turks. The Emperor asked him what time it would require to take Belgrade? " It would require fifteen days with a formidable army, obedient officers, and provided that no fault was committed." General Lacy exclaimed, that he would take it in two days. " Let us leave it (the Emperor replied) to Laudon, he has been their already.

The Empress of Russia means to send a fleet of 24 sail of the line into the Mediterranean; and the Gazette of Petersburgh, published by royal authority, declares that no opposition will be made to the entrance of this force into the Mediterranean, either by France or England, in the latter of which, it has been agreed this fleet shall victual and refit.

General Field Mareschal Laudon, well known for his military talents, and determined bravery in the war of 1757, undertakes, at the age of 70, the conquest of Moldavia, while the Emperor in person takes upon him the command of the army in Hungary, consisting of 200,000 men, which being divided into different bodies, will attack the Turks in Servia, Bulgaria, and Bosnia.

A third army will be stationed in Galicia, which with the Russians, who are to join it, will amount to 80,000 men, and can with great facility act in concert with the grand army of the Empress, which is already on the borders of the Ukraine, and of Podolia.

It is resolved to enter Moldavia by two armies, at two different places at the same time; the Austrian forces will penetrate into it by Buckowine, and the Russians by the Polish Ukraine.

Extract of a Letter from Langeac, Lower Auvergne, Jan. 25.

" An enterprizing Swiss has made his appearance here, who pretends to have invented an instrument of war, which will discharge 300 balls in the space of three minutes, that ten people, with this instrument, will do as much execution as a whole regiment. He is to make an experiment in the course of a fortnight. He comes from Fribourg. Being asked why he did not make tryal of his instrument there, he answered, " That it would have cost him his life." He has been in several actions, and has many fears about him.

There is said to be now living in Paris, in a very low degree, a woman of extraordinary high rank. Her name is Cecilia; she calls herself the daughter of Achmet III. Emperor of the Turks, and says she was born in the year 1710 of the Christian æra. Her life has been published at Paris, and though it has the air of a romance, it is said to be genuine. The publisher says, she lives in the *Rue de la Harpe*, at the College of Bayeux, where she may be seen every day. She is described as a woman respectable for her years, her good sense, her fortitude, her piety, and her charities, notwithstanding the smallness of her fortune. If all this be true, a people of credit vouch for it, one cannot be too much

Vol. III.
50642

CONSTANTINOPLE, 29 *Décembre.*

LE Grand Seigneur a déclaré le Capitaine Pacha, Grand Amiral de la Mer Noire, & Généralissime des troupes de cette partie des possessions Ottomanes. Cette distinction n'est pas moins due à son mérite, qu'à l'argent qu'il a apporté d'Egypte au trésor public, qui à ce qu'on dit monte à plus de cinquante millions de piastres, sans y comprendre 6,000,000 qu'il avoit envoyé auparavant. On dit que sa premiere entreprise sera une descente dans la Crimée, au printemps prochain, avec un corps de 25,000 hommes choisis, pour tacher de prendre cette Presqu'Isle aux Russes.

LONDRES, 1 Février.

Il est certain que Laudon, Maréchal-de-Camp commandera une armée contre les Turcs. L'Empereur lui ayant demandé combien il falloit de temps pour prendre Belgrade, il répondit 15 jours, avec une armée formidable, des Officiers obéissans, & pourvu qu'on ne fasse aucune faute. Le Général Lacy s'écria qu'il la prendroit en deux jours. "Remettons là, (repartit l'Empereur) à Laudon, il y a déjà été.

L'Impératrice de Russie a dessein d'envoyer une flotte de 24 vaisseaux de ligne à la Méditerranée, & la Gazette de Petersbourgh, publiée par autorité royale, déclare que son entrée dans la Méditerranée sera permise, tant par la France que par l'Angleterre; c'est ici où on a convenu d'avitailler & reparer la flotte.

Le Général Laudon, Maréchal-de-Camp, bien connu par les talens militaires, & sa bravoure déterminée dans la guerre de 1757, entreprend, à l'âge de 70 ans, la conquête de la Moldavie, pendant que l'Empereur en personne se charge du commandement de l'armée en Hongrie, qui consiste en 200,000 hommes, laquelle étant divisée en différens corps, attaquera les Turcs dans la Servie, Bulgarie & Bosnie.

Il y aura une troisième armée dans la Galicie, qui avec les Russes qui doivent la joindre, sera de 80,000 hommes, & elle peut très-aisément agir de concert avec la grande armée de l'Impératrice, qui est déjà sur les bords de l'Ukraine & de la Podolie.

On a résolu d'entrer dans la Moldavie par deux armées à différens endroits; les troupes Autrichiennes y pénétreront par Buckowine, & celle des Russes par l'Ukraine Polonoise.

Extrait d'une Lettre de Langeac, Basse Auvergne, 25 Janvier.

Un Suisse entreprenant, actuélement en cette ville, se flatte d'avoir inventé une machine de guerre, qui déchargera 300 balles dans l'espace de trois minutes, que dix hommes avec cet instrument feront autant d'exécution que tout un Régiment. Il doit en faire l'épreuve dans quinze jours. Il vient de Fribourg. Après lui avoir demandé pourquoi il n'en avoit pas fait l'essai, il répondit que cela lui auroit couté la vie. Il s'est trouvé dans plusieurs actions, & a sur lui plusieurs cicatrices.

On dit qu'il y a actuélement à Paris, dans un état fort médiocre, une femme d'un très-haut rang. Elle se nomme Cecile, & se dit fille d'Achmet III. Empereur des Turcs, & qu'elle naquit en l'année 1710 de l'ere Chrétienne. On a publié sa vie à Paris, & quoi qu'elle ait l'air d'un Roman, on dit qu'elle est véritable. L'Editeur dit qu'elle demeure dans la rue de la Harpe, au Collége de Bayeux, où l'on peut la voir tous les jours. On la représente comme une femme respectable par son âge, son bon sens, son courage, sa piété & les charités, non-obstant la médiocrité de sa fortune. Si tout cela est vrai, comme des gens dignes de foi l'assurent, on sçauroit trop s'étonner des caprices de la fortune.

Tom III.

The first page of the Montreal *Gazette* for June 5, 1788.
At this time, the newspaper was bilingual.

make a living, and from their shop came a number of "firsts": the first Canadian almanac (1765), another staple of the early printers; the first book in English (*The Trial of Daniel Disney*, 1767); the first book in an Indian language (a collection of prayers and other devotional works in Montagnais, also 1767); and the first book of Canadian poetry, Thomas Cary's *Abram's Plains* (1789). The latter was printed at Cary's expense, as were most literary works until a much later period, and appeared only a week before Brown's death on March 22. Gilmore had died of alcoholism in 1773.

Brown and Gilmore printed not only in English and Montagnais, but also in French; and it is worth remarking that the separation of English and French publishing is a development that came only a good deal later. For practical reasons a printer-publisher was unlikely to want to restrict his business along language lines: business was business, and it was scarce enough for the early printers not to be able to specialize even had they wished to. But in fact most of them were educated and often bilingual, and could as readily write and edit copy (in several languages) as set type and work the press. There is something emblematic about the fact that the oldest English-language newspaper in Canada, the Montreal

Gazette, was founded by Fleury Mesplet (1734-94), a printer from France (by way of London and Philadelphia) who, on commission from Benjamin Franklin, had printed in 1774 a pamphlet addressed "To the Inhabitants of the Province of Quebec" which tried to entice the latter into joining the Thirteen Colonies.

The cultural and political matrix out of which publishing in Quebec emerged was full of paradoxes and conflicts of this kind. Mesplet's paper was in fact founded as a French-language paper, the *Gazette du commerce et littéraire* (1778 — the seemingly awkward combination of commercial and literary news was normal for the times). This *Gazette* lasted for only one year, when Mesplet and his editor Valentin Jautard were imprisoned on Governor Sir Frederick Haldimand's orders for criticizing the judiciary. For three years the two men shared a prison cell with two other detainees "and a considerable number of mice." Mesplet later founded a second newspaper, the *Gazette de Montréal*, which was first French, latterly bilingual, and finally English.

Mesplet came to Montreal with Montgomery's occupying forces in 1776, and was left behind when the Americans retreated. This inauspicious start to his career in Canada was a forecast of worse to come, and one scholar has characterized Mesplet's eighteen years in Montreal as "a record of failure, disappointments, and disgrace," as his Enlightenment principles led to predictable clashes with the authorities. But he did set up the first printing press in the city of Montreal, and his shop on rue Nôtre-Dame was something of an intellectual hang-out in the best tradition of European printers. Much of his bread-and-butter work came from religious and modest governmental commissions, including, for example, his first publication, a book of rules for a Sulpician mutual benefit society (*Règlement de la confrerie de l'Adoration perpétuelle du S. Sacrement et de la bonne mort*, 1776) and *The Manual Exercise* (1787) prepared for the Adjutant-General's office. At his death in 1794, his type and presses passed at auction to Edward Edwards (1756-1816), who also became the publisher of the *Gazette*. Edwards was otherwise a modest printer only, and an edition of Aesop's fables in Robert Dodsley's popular eighteenth-century English translation (1800) was his only substantial publication.

After William Brown's death at Quebec City in 1789, his business passed to Brown's nephew Samuel Neilson, who brought his younger brother John over from Scot-

land to assist him. At Samuel's death in early 1793 at
only twenty-three, the seventeen-year-old John inherited the company, which over the next few decades he
would transform into the largest book business (printing, publishing, bookselling, binding etc.) in British
North America. More than half of all of the books published in Quebec between 1800 and 1820 came from
Neilson's presses, and James Brown, a Montreal printer
who founded the first Canadian paper mill at Saint-André
d'Argenteuil in 1804, once remarked that Neilson was
"the largest consumer of paper in this country." Neilson
was the first printer to print music in Canada, and the
Neilson firm published Quebec's first magazine, the
bilingual *Quebec Magazine/Le Magasin de Québec* (1792-
94). Like most Canadian magazines until the mid-nine-
teenth century, the *Quebec Magazine* was not a financial
success; the population base was too small to support
such ventures. Yet the Neilsons were among the first
(only *The Nova-Scotia Magazine* was earlier) in a long line
of cultural enthusiasts in the Canadian book trade who
were willing to lose money on literary projects which
they considered good for the country.

A few other English printers opened shops in eighteenth-century Quebec, including William Moore and

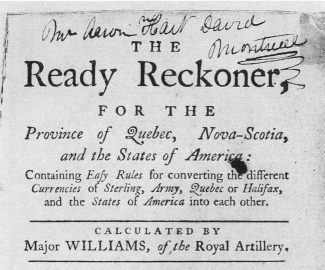

Mr Aaron Hart David Montreal

THE
Ready Reckoner,

FOR THE
Province of Quebec, Nova-Scotia, and the States of America:
Containing *Eafy Rules* for converting the different Currencies of *Sterling, Army, Quebec* or *Halifax*, and the *States* of *America* into each other.

CALCULATED BY
Major WILLIAMS, *of the* Royal Artillery.

TO WHICH ARE ADDED A
A TABLE OF THE WEIGHT OF GOLD COIN,
With its VALUE in *Quebec* or *Halifax*, reduced to *Dollars, Livres & Sous.*

AND AN EASY
TABLE OF GRAINS FROM 1 TO 1000,
With their *Sum* in *Quebec* Currency.

Quebec: *Printed* by WM. MOORE,
AT THE
HERALD PRINTING-OFFICE, 1790.

An early "reckoner," used to calculate currency values at a time when a number of different currencies were in use in North America. The book, printed in Quebec City by William Moore in 1790, survives in only two copies.

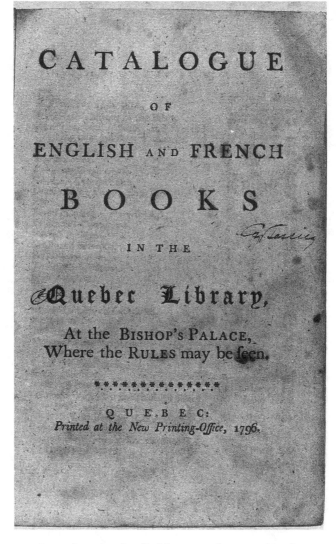

CATALOGUE

OF

ENGLISH AND FRENCH

BOOKS

IN THE

𝔔uebec 𝔏ibrary,

At the BISHOP's PALACE,
Where the RULES may be seen.

* * * * * * * * * * * * * *

QUEBEC:
Printed at the New Printing-Office, 1796.

An early example of a library catalogue, printed at
the Neilson shop in Quebec City in 1796.

William Vondenvelden, but their careers were short by comparison with those of Brown and Gilmore, the Neilsons, and Fleury Mesplet. The colony was too small to support a printing and publishing industry on any but a tiny scale. Original publishing in the modern sense — acquiring manuscripts and publishing them on a royalty basis — did not exist, and the minuscule amount of literary and general publishing that did occur was always carried out at the author's expense, usually by subscription.

That there was a literary culture in the province is undeniable. Men like François-Étienne Cugnet, Louis Guillaume Verner, and Claude-Thomas Dupuy (the *intendant* from 1725-28) had large libraries which were not limited to theology, law, and the classics, and a public subscription library was established at the Bishop's Palace in Quebec City as early as 1779. By 1796, when its second printed catalogue was issued, one could go there to borrow the works of Hume, Locke, Rousseau, Voltaire and other controversial writers, in either English or French, from among some 2,700 volumes. The Quebec Library (as it was called) existed until 1869, when it was absorbed into the Literary and Historical Society of Quebec (founded in 1824 and still active).

Books were imported from Europe and the United States for sale mainly to the educated elite. A single surviving copy of John Neilson's earliest book catalogue, issued in 1800, lists a stock of some 265 titles, 80 per cent in English and 16 per cent in French (the remaining books were in Latin and Italian). This copy is annotated by Neilson himself, and from his scribbles we can picture Jacob Mountain, the Anglican Bishop of Quebec, purchasing a biographical dictionary, and the Quebec Library sending for the works of Racine in French. The smaller proportion of books available in French can likely be explained by the fact that the Napoleonic Wars had interrupted trade between Canada and France. Certainly the normal demand for books in both languages was likely to have been more or less equal.

At the close of the eighteenth century, then, printing had been established in Quebec City and Montreal, and a rudimentary trade in books was in place. Even with the simple technology available to them, the early Canadian printers were capable of producing large-scale works, such as the *Édits* of 1803-06 printed by Pierre-Édouard Desbarats (in whose business Neilson had a financial stake), a two-volume collection of over 1,000 pages, or William Smith's 700-page *History of Canada*,

PRINTING.

GEORGE J. WRIGHT respectfully acquaints his friends and the public, that he has commenced Printing at No. 2, St. Genevieve Street, facing the Government Gardens, and solicits a share of their favors in his line.

G. J. WRIGHT flatters himself that having a perfect knowledge of his profession, and being furnished with an elegant assortment of materials suitable for printing of every description, he will be enabled to render entire satisfaction to all who may favor him with their encouragement.

QUEBEC, 17th Aug. 1816.

George J. Wright was one of several printers who opened shops in Quebec City in the second decade of the nineteenth century. As only a single sermon is known with his imprint, his business probably did not flourish.

printed for the author by Neilson and published in 1815. It is, however, in the nineteenth century that English publishing in Quebec gradually assumes a more modern shape, as an increasing population and developments in education (and especially literacy) begin to transform the book trade.

CB

In Canada as elsewhere where printing was established, technological change in the printing trade during the nineteenth century completely altered the traditional processes of making books. Only a century after Brown and Gilmore opened their modest printing office, John Lovell was operating a plant in Montreal which held twelve steam-operated presses and employed 150 people. The vast quantity of paper necessary to feed such a large operation was now made from trees (chemically rendered wood pulp) rather than from rags. Type was cast by machine, and by the 1860s the Montreal Type Foundry was using nine such casters. Even wood type, long used for posters and other display work, was being cut mechanically by a company in Hamilton, Ontario. Towards the end of the century machines were developed for setting type (the Merganthaler linotype machine being the best known), making the laborious job of setting each letter by hand a thing of the past. Earlier in the century the use of stereotype plates made the production of large quantities of a book or newspaper a much simpler matter. In less than a century, the industry had changed almost beyond recognition. When the Numismatic and Antiquarian Society of Montreal sponsored a celebration in 1877 to mark the 400th anniversary of the introduction of printing into England by William Caxton, two of its themes were "the progress which has been made in printing" and "the progress of the Art in Canada."

English publishing in nineteenth-century Quebec paralleled, then, the development of the printing and publishing trades elsewhere, though the size of the colony and its slow growth, as well as the even slower growth of a literary culture, were special factors. During the first twenty-five years of the new century progress was slow, and only gradually did new names begin to appear in the imprints of books and newspapers. The functions of printer, publisher, and bookseller began slowly to separate, and by the 1820s bookselling was a distinct activity in Montreal. The younger printers followed the earlier pattern: James Brown (*The Canadian Gazette*), William Gray (*The Montreal Herald*), Ariel Bowman (*The Sun*), Nahum Mower (*The Canadian Courant and Montreal Advertiser*), and Thomas Cary (*The Quebec Mercury*) all attempted to base their firms in part on the publication of a newspaper, with varying degrees of success. All of these printers carried out work in both languages, though James Brown worked mainly in French and Nahum Mower (who went to Montreal from Vermont in 1807) worked predominantly in English. The Neilson shop in Quebec City remained the largest firm until well into the century, but Montreal's increasing importance as the centre for the Quebec book trade corresponded to the city's commercial dominance.

As the number of printers and booksellers grew, the occasional evidence of a local literature also surfaced, mainly in the genre of poetry. Ann Cuthbert Knight (née Rae, later Fleming) published two collections of poems in Edinburgh around the time she settled permanently in Montreal in 1815 (one of them, *A Year in Canada and Other Poems*, grew out of an earlier trip). Once settled, she opened a school (examples survive of her using her own publications as prize books) and turned her attention to writing school books. Ariel

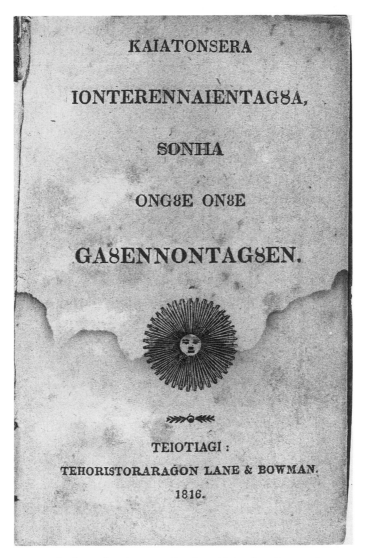

A little Mohawk prayer book published in Montreal
(Teiotiagi) in 1816. The translator was P. Joseph Marcoux,
and this copy belonged to the printer James Lane.

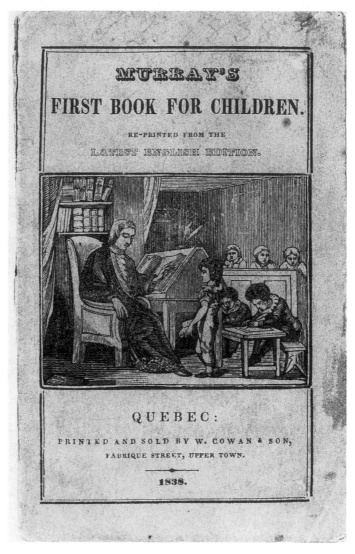

MURRAY'S

FIRST BOOK FOR CHILDREN.

RE-PRINTED FROM THE

LATEST ENGLISH EDITION.

QUEBEC:

PRINTED AND SOLD BY W. COWAN & SON,
FABRIQUE STREET, UPPER TOWN.

1838.

A Canadian reprint of an English alphabet book
and first reader for children, issued in
Quebec City in 1838.

Bowman, already referred to as a printer, published his own *Hours of Childhood and Other Poems* in 1820. Margaret Blennerhassett, originally from Ireland, came to Canada from the United States. (She and her husband fled to Montreal after being involved in Aaron Burr's political conspiracies in the Louisiana Territories). Her collection The *Widow of the Rock and Other Poems* (1824) was the earliest book of poems by a woman to be published in Canada. Other early books of this kind include collections by Levi Adams, William F. Hawley, Adam Kidd, and Standish O'Grady. All of them were printed by Montreal printers but published by the authors, who would canvas sufficient subscriptions in advance to meet the costs of production.

Subscription publishing was relatively common in the case of books which a publisher could not risk, or where a book was too expensive to produce without raising significant capital in advance. Examples of subscription register books which survive from the nineteenth century show that these were often placed in a prominent bookstore where potential customers were likely to pass by. Advertisements would also be inserted in newspapers, and doubtless then as now the author's friends would in particular be persuaded to sign up for a copy or two. In England or France the list of subscribers' names would frequently be printed and included in the published book, though this practice was rare in Canada (*St. Ursula's Convent*, the first novel by a native-born Canadian to be published in Canada, being a notable exception). Adam Kidd is supposed to have sold subscriptions for his 1830 book *The Huron Chief and Other Poems* door-to-door in Montreal, and he claimed in the preface that the "liberal and friendly encouragement with which my first attempt has been so highly favoured, and particularly in the Canadas" actually translated into 1,500 subscriptions. This is a very large number for the time, as it is unlikely that any literary work published in Canada before mid-century sold much more than 500 copies, the average being probably somewhat fewer.

Not until almost the end of the century did subscription publishing die out. *Selections from Canadian Poets*, the first anthology of Canadian poetry, edited by Edward Hartley Dewart, was printed on a subscription basis by John Lovell in 1864. The imprints on literary works sometimes disguise what was in fact vanity publishing. J.B. Waid of Bleury Street in Montreal, who styled himself the Bard of Niagara, brought out a book of prose and poetry entitled *Variety* in 1872. The title-page describes it as "Printed By John Lovell," the "printed by" being a sure indication that if it was not published by subscription then the author certainly paid for it himself. The frontispiece, if one can term it thus, provides confirmation: within a ruled frame are the words "Space for a Picture of the Bard, which J.G. Parks [a local photographer] will insert for 25 cents." Variations such as "published for the trade" and the more honest "printed for the author" are common. The impressive imprint on R.J. MacGeorge's *Tales, Sketches and Lyrics* of 1858 (Toronto: A.H. Armour & Co.; James Bain; Wm. Caverhill; J.C. Geikie; Maclear & Co.; H. Rowsell; Thompson & Co.; Wiman & Co., Wholesale Agents) does not mean that all of these men fought to have a piece of the book at a nineteenth-century version of an auction of rights. The book was printed for the author by Lovell; the other names are meant simply to inform the public where copies could be bought.

MacGeorge was a serious man, and in his brief preface he expresses sentiments with which, were they somewhat less grandiloquent and moralistic, a twentieth-century publisher of poetry and serious fiction might well agree. He says that the object of one of his tales is to ridicule the inordinate lust for the perusal of slip-slop romances, which so signally prevails at present in "this Canada." Truly alarming is the extent of the epidemic, and unless checked, it cannot fail to visit the rising generation with psychologic emasculation and discrepitness.

The serious nineteenth-century Canadian writer, no less than her or his twentieth-century counterpart, did not enjoy the fruits of fame and a large market, and publishers on the whole could not risk their money in publishing indigenous writers whose sales would be very small. The public response to Major John Richardson's novel *The Canadian Brothers*, which Armour and Ramsay of Montreal brought out in 1840, was minimal despite generally favourable reviews. Richardson wanted the first edition to be published in Canada, but he later remarked that "I might as well have done so in Kamtschatka," so poor were sales.

The copyright laws were an additional impediment to a Canadian publishing industry, for there was nothing to prevent a British or American publisher from pirating a Canadian book and issuing it without any payment of royalties. Writers of merit like Thomas Chandler Haliburton and Susannah Moodie therefore published

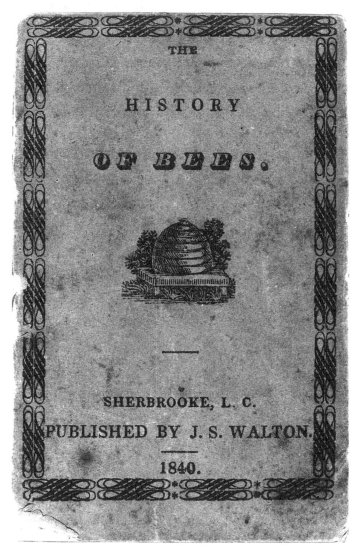

THE

HISTORY

OF BEES.

SHERBROOKE, L. C.

PUBLISHED BY J. S. WALTON.

1840.

This sixteen-page pamphlet is an early example of an
Eastern Townships imprint. It is illustrated with
several woodcuts.

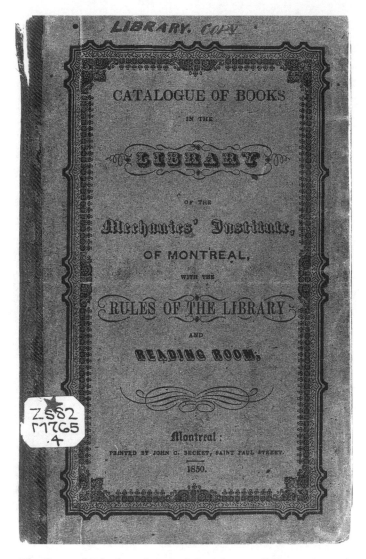

CATALOGUE OF BOOKS

IN THE

LIBRARY

OF THE

Mechanics' Institute,

OF MONTREAL,

WITH THE

RULES OF THE LIBRARY

AND

READING ROOM,

Montreal:

PRINTED BY JOHN C. BECKET, SAINT PAUL STREET.

1850.

The first published catalogue of the Library of the Mechanics'
Institute (1850), now the Atwater Library. This copy
belonged to John Redpath, the first president of the
Mechanics' Institute.

their books in London in order to ensure that they would be remunerated. On the other hand, a number of nineteenth-century English publishers in Quebec, like their confreres in Toronto, were in fact thieves, though thieves of a legally sanctioned sort. This is so because the same copyright laws which permitted an English publisher like Richard Bentley to reprint Haliburton's *The Clockmaker* without permission could not prevent a Montreal publisher from issuing a work by Charles Dickens or Mark Twain with equal impunity.

Twain's Canadian publisher, Dawson Brothers of Montreal, were not pirates of this sort, but they and Twain fought a long battle against rivals who did fly the Jolly Roger. The fact that unauthorized printings of his books were being issued by Canadian publishers was irritating to Twain; but more than that, he was infuriated by the fact that these cheap reprints were then being sold in the United States, thus seriously cutting into the market for the authorized American editions. Twain visited Montreal on several occasions so as to be on British soil when the Dawson Brothers edition of one of his books was published, it being one of the oddities of the copyright laws that the author be there, as it were, to catch the books as they fell from the casing machine in order to secure copyright. It was on such a visit in 1881, in the company of a Boston publisher, that he replied to a suggestion that the publisher's presence might have something to do with a recent diamond theft: "No, possibly not: the burglar took the diamond studs, but left the shirt; only a reformed Toronto publisher would have left the shirt." The trade in unauthorized reprints was briskest in Toronto, but the otherwise reputable John Lovell and other Montreal publishers like Richard Worthington engaged in it as well.

Reprints of American and British books in fact became one of the staples of the Montreal publishers during the period from roughly mid-century until 1891, when changes in copyright legislation ended the practice to a large extent. Co-existing with the pirated books were legitimate (i.e., paid for) Canadian editions of a host of British and American authors. Dawson Brothers published George Eliot and Twain among others, and the publication of the Dawson edition of *Huckleberry Finn* was what brought Twain to Montreal in February of 1885, when he signed a copy of the book for George Iles, the manager of the Windsor Hotel on Peel Street where he stayed. The reprint industry, legitimate or otherwise, fed the reading public's enormous appetite

OBSERVATIONS

ON

THE RIGHTS

OF THE

BRITISH COLONIES

TO

Representation

IN THE

IMPERIAL PARLIAMENT,

BY

DAVID CHISHOLME.

Pulchrum est bene facere Reipublicæ.

THREE-RIVERS:
PRINTED AND PUBLISHED BY G. STOBBS,
AND SOLD BY ALL BOOKSELLERS.

—

1832.

David Chisholme (1796-1842) was a government official
when Stobbs issued this substantial work of 336 pages.
Chisholme was later the editor of the Montreal
Gazette and the Montreal *Herald*.

A rare pamphlet on hypnotism, originally published in the
United States and reissued in Montreal by the author
in 1844.

for fiction by the popular authors of the day and provided a steady income to many Quebec publishers. It is no accident that the death of this facet of the trade in the 1890s coincides with a great decline in English-Quebec publishing at the end of the century.

☙

But let us return to the earlier period, the second third of the nineteenth century, when a number of important English-language publishers came on the scene and publishing spread to the smaller centres. English-language printing and publishing had taken place mainly in Montreal since the decline of the Neilson shop, but there were English printers in the Eastern Townships as early as the 1820s. J.S. Walton, first in Stanstead and subsequently in Sherbrooke, produced school books as well as the usual job printing. At Three Rivers, George Stobbs published *The Christian Sentinel and Anglo-Canadian Churchman's Magazine* in 1830-31, and thereafter was active as a job-printer, producing among other things an edition in 1833 for the author of James Russell's *Matilda, or the Indian's Captive*, a rare Canadian example of the Indian captivity narrative, a genre popular in the

United States. Stobbs and Walton were, however, scarcely publishers in the modern sense, and local publishing in English in the province outside of Montreal has been, and still is, mainly of the demand or vanity sort.

A representative Montreal publisher of the time on the older model (i.e., a bookseller-publisher) was Henry H. Cunningham (d. 1853), whose bookshop was first on rue St-Paul and later on Nôtre-Dame. He began to publish books as early as 1810, and did so sporadically for almost forty years, one of his last books being Major Richardson's *The Guards in Canada*, which appeared in 1848, five years before Cunningham's death.He published school books as well as a magazine, *The Canadian Review and Literary and Historical Magazine*, but also other books more characteristic of a modern trade publisher: John Perrin's *The Elements of French Conversation* (1810), an edition of Byron's *Poems on His Domestic Circumstances* (1816), the intriguingly anonymous *The Mysteries of Montreal: A Novel Founded on Facts* (1846 — "'Blast this wind and rain! A body can be surprised and despatched in this delightful spot without being aware of his murderer's approach,'" it begins, à la Bulwer Lytton), and Richardson's *Eight Years in Canada* (1847).

Montreal publisher Rollo Campbell (1803-71),
reproduced from J. Douglas Borthwick,
Montreal, Its History (1875).

Montreal publisher Robert Miller (b. 1819),
reproduced from J. Douglas Borthwick,
Montreal, Its History (1875).

Among other men active in the Montreal book trade in the 1830s and 1840s were Rollo Campbell, Robert and Adam Miller, Andrew Armour and Hew Ramsay, and John Lovell. Campbell (1803-71) began as a printer for the Montreal *Gazette*, and eventually established one of the largest printing businesses in Quebec. He first printed and later owned *The Pilot* (1844-62), a reform newspaper, and he himself became involved in city politics. His name occurs frequently in the imprints of Montreal publications in the 1830s, 40s, and 50s, and he had a branch office in Quebec City as well. Most of these books, however, were printed by him on behalf of other publishers. R. & A. Miller were also active in the 1840s and 50s, after which their business moved to Toronto, where they had maintained a branch for some time. They were long the publishers, among other books, of *The Strangers' Guide to the Cities of Montreal and Quebec*, and they were also active as schoolbook publishers. Armour & Ramsay were important booksellers and textbook publishers, as well as binders and job printers. Hew Ramsay continued the business on his own from the rue St-François-Xavier premises after the partnership broke up in 1851. Among the many books that bear the Armour & Ramsay imprint are Richardson's

Personal Memoirs (1838) and *The Canadian Brothers* (1840).

One of the earliest examples of an American publisher establishing a Canadian branch was D. & J. Sadlier & Co., the New York-based Catholic publishing house whose Montreal office at the corner of Nôtre-Dame and St-François-Xavier was opened in 1848-49. James Sadlier's wife, the novelist Mary Anne Sadlier, had emigrated to Montreal from Ireland in 1844 before moving on to the United States, where her immensely popular but now largely forgotten novels were published. She was a friend of Thomas D'Arcy McGee and edited his posthumous *Poems* (1869), "these scattered remains of a genius all too soon extinguished in death," as she called them. The Sadliers imported and stocked large numbers of books (including their own publications, of course, most of which have a secondary Montreal imprint), textbooks, maps, prints, and stationery, and within five years they were claiming to have "the largest & best selected stock...to be found in Canada."

John Lovell (1810-93) was the most important nineteenth-century publisher not only in Montreal, but indeed in Canada as a whole, and his influence in the United States was also significant. His home, on the site where The Bay department store now rises at the

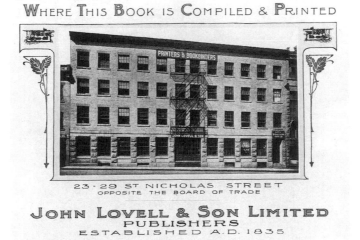

WHERE THIS BOOK IS COMPILED & PRINTED

23 - 29 ST NICHOLAS STREET
OPPOSITE THE BOARD OF TRADE

JOHN LOVELL & SON LIMITED
PUBLISHERS
ESTABLISHED A.D. 1835

A typical John Lovell advertisement, this one from the
Lovell Montreal city directory for 1925-26.

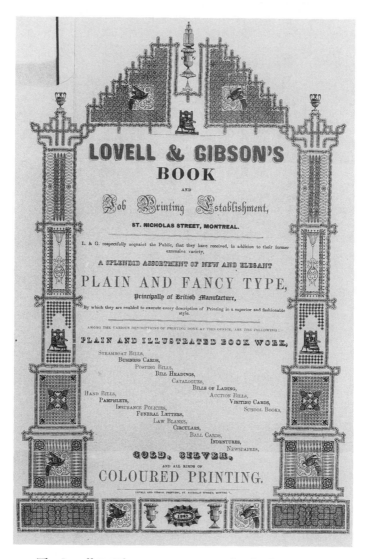

The Lovell & Gibson type specimen book of 1847 is an
impressive example of the genre. The printing plant on
St. Nicholas Street offered a vast array of type fonts and
illustrative cuts and ornaments, and the specimen book
itself is printed in several colours.

corner of Ste-Catherine and Union, attracted the literati and all manner of people from the worlds of publishing and politics. Jefferson Davis visited when he came to Canada in 1867 after his trial and presidential pardon. Lovell began as a printer's apprentice in 1823, and his career paralleled — indeed defined — the golden years of English publishing in Quebec. The company started by him is still active, although his death coincided almost exactly with a decline in English publishing in the province, not that his death was the cause of it. Hundreds, even thousands of books bear his imprint, from slim pamphlets to the massive *Canadian Dominion Directory* of 1871, which at 2,562 pages is probably the largest single volume issued by a Canadian publisher until well into this century.

Lovell worked his way up to prominence only gradually from rural Irish roots. A partnership with John Gibson, his brother-in-law, led to innovations in the trade such as *The Literary Garland*, the first Canadian literary magazine to pay contributors, and *Snow Drop*, the earliest Canadian children's magazine. (At the end of the first volume, the editor, Eliza Cushing, noted that "while we receive many expressions of warm approbation, we regret to say that our subscription list is still so small, that we should hardly feel justified in continuing the publication, had we not reason to believe that our present subscribers will continue their patronage, and that successful efforts will be made to increase the number for the coming year" — sentiments with which many a later Canadian magazine editor could only nod sadly in agreement). By the 1850s, the Lovell and Gibson firm had offices in Toronto and Quebec City as well as Montreal, and an increasing number of books — novels, poetry, city directories (including the directory for Montreal begun by Robert Mackay), schoolbooks, and Canadian editions of American and British titles — flowed from the Lovell presses (Gibson having died in 1850). Copyright complications eventually led him to build a plant in the United States just over the Quebec-New York state border, as well as to establish a branch in New York City under his son's management. The company name went through a number of changes and finally stabilized in 1884 as John Lovell and Son.

Lovell was the last important English printer-publisher in Quebec. Specialization in the trade had taken on its modern form by the end of the century, and the new publishing houses which arose between 1890 and

1914 were publishers and publishers only. The Ryerson Press in Toronto alone carried on in Canada as a major trade publisher with its own printing plant until 1970, and not surprisingly its roots were deep in the nineteenth century. After John Lovell's death the firm he founded continued to publish, but its output shrank considerably and consisted mainly of specialized works like city directories and street guides.

☙

At mid-century and even later, Montreal was the centre of the Canadian book trade in both English and French. It has remained so for books in French, but by the turn of the century the publishing and distribution of books in English had shifted to Toronto, and Quebec had declined greatly as a publishing centre. In the period roughly from Confederation to 1900 several new publishers came on the scene in Montreal, but most of them were booksellers who also published books. Richard Worthington, for example, published a number of interesting books in the 1860s including an English translation of François-Xavier Garneau's *Histoire du Canada* and Robert Christie's *History of the Late Province of Lower Canada*, both in 1866. Worthington later moved his publishing activities to New York City.

Not far from Worthington's shop at 235 rue St-Jacques, in both directions, were two other important bookseller-publishers, William Drysdale at No. 232 (established 1874, later at No. 240) and F.E. Grafton at No. 250 (established 1865). One of the first books published by Drysdale was Borthwick's *Montreal* (1875), an elaborate photographic "who's who" sort of book that still has value for biographical and historical research. Drysdale's output increased significantly in the 1880s and 1890s and covered fields from history and religion to medicine, natural history, literature, and even a cookbook. W.D. Lighthall's novel *The Young Seigneur* was issued pseudonymously by Drysdale in 1888, and Watson Griffin, then an editorial writer for the Montreal *Star*, wrote to the publisher to say that he had "sat up late last night to read with keen interest your book, *The Young Seigneur,* and after finishing it dreamed about it until morning." Grafton started earlier and lasted longer—the business closed in 1918, whereas Drysdale went out of business in 1906—but his publications, somewhat fewer than Drysdale's, covered a similar range.

William Drysdale was an important bookseller-publisher
in Montreal in the last quarter of the nineteenth century.
Reproduced from George L. Parker,
The Beginnings of the Book Trade in Canda (1985).

In the early 1890s, a number of foreign publishers opened offices in Canada. In the twenty-five years before World War I, Macmillan, Hodder and Stoughton, Oxford University Press, and several others began Canadian branches, and all chose Toronto rather than Montreal. New indigenous houses such as George N. Morang and McClelland and Goodchild (later McClelland and Stewart) also worked out of Toronto, with the result that English publishing in Quebec declined substantially and never quite regained the level of prominance it had in the nineteenth century.

Lovell's city directory for 1913-14 lists twenty-one entries under "Publishers," of which eleven are French. Of the remaining ten most are inconsequential (e.g. the International Hotel Register Co.), only John Dougall and Son (publishers of the *Witness* and other papers), Lovell, and Sadlier being of any importance. But even they, at that point, were scarcely trade publishers in the fullest sense, and all were as dependent on the printing or bookselling business as on publishing properly speaking. A decade later the list is certainly longer, but aside from branches of J.B. Lippincott (an American house) and the Grolier Society, little more trade publishing was taking place than had gone on before the

60

war. An exception was the Renouf Publishing Co.,
which evolved from Dawson Bros. Although Renouf
published the occasional literary title, such as J.C.
Hodgson's 1935 novel *Lion & Lily*, the company was
better known as an important scientific and governmental publisher. Mention should be made also of a
number of large-scale printing businesses which
sometimes acted as publishers: The Gazette Printing
Co. (whose imprint is on Stephen Leacock's first book
of humour, *Literary Lapses*, though the book was privately
published), The Montreal Star Publishing Company,
Consolidated Press, The Canadian Railroaders Ltd.,
Garden City Press (in Ste- Anne-de-Bellevue), and C.C.
Ronalds, whose annual Christmas books are still
remembered.

The first post-war Montreal trade publisher of note
was Louis Carrier (1898-1961), whose father was
French and mother English. He fought in the air at the
end of World War I and then became a journalist, initially
for the *Telegraph* in Quebec City and subsequently for
both the *Gazette* and the *Star* in Montreal. A very few
books from the mid-twenties, in both languages, bear
his imprint (or the imprint of the Mercury Press, which
he also used), and by 1927 he was beginning to create a

more extensive list. Some sixteen books were in print by that year, including a book of poems by Paul Gouin entitled *Médailles anciennes: poèmes historiques*. Gouin was a lawyer and son of a former prime minister of Quebec, Sir Lorimer Gouin. On the latter's death in 1929, Paul Gouin inherited some money and joined Carrier in the publishing business. Carrier had also hired David Legate away from the *Star* to do editorial work. Legate, later Stephen Leacock's biographer, remembered "sitting pretty in an office of my own, carpet on the floor, marble inkstand on the desk and straining mightily to look like an editor." In his memoirs he also recounts an amusing story of attempting to sell American rights to a novel by Louis Arthur Cunningham, *This Thing Called Love*. Legate went to New York well armed with bootleg gin and set up at the Commodore Hotel. "The gin or the excitement" caused him to pass out, which understandably did not make a good impression on the assembled gods of American publishing.

Carrier published extensively in 1928 and 1929, and Frederick Philip Grove and Sir Andrew Macphail were among the authors on his list. Grove stayed with Carrier during the Montreal stop of his 1928-29 lecture tour, and once suggested that Carrier try to acquire

THE
STORIED STREETS
OF QUEBEC

By BLODWEN DAVIES

Illustrations by
ROBERT PILOT
A. R. C. A.

LOUIS CARRIER & CO
AT THE MERCURY
MONTREAL
NEW YORK   LONDON

The title-page of a Louis Carrier book, issued in 1929
in a signed and numbered edition of 950 copies.

Graphic Press in Ottawa (for whom Grove later worked) from its owner, Henry Miller. Carrier's publishing house was similar in some ways to the more famous Graphic: both were founded about the same time, both were forced into bankruptcy by the Depression about the same time (Carrier in 1931), and both took pride in the design and production of their books. Carrier, however, published non-Canadian as well as Canadian books and had a remarkably bilingual and bicultural list, perhaps the last Canadian publisher, aside from the Queen's/King's Printer, to do so. He maintained an office in New York, and his partner Alan Isles looked after U.S. sales. (Watson Kirkconnell's *The North American Book of Icelandic Verse*, issued in 1930, bears the imprint "Louis Carrier & Alan Isles, Inc., New York & Montreal." Kirkconnell, who at that time was teaching classics at Wesley College in Winnipeg, had been recommended to Carrier by Grove.)

With Carrier's disappearance from the scene, English publishing in Quebec almost fell from sight again. The newspaper presses, such as the three English dailies in Montreal and the *Chronicle-Telegraph* in Quebec City, produced books from time to time. The first book by the poet Alfred Bailey, for example, *Songs of the Saguenay*

and Other Poems, was published by the Chronicle-Telegraph Publishing Company in 1927; and as the editor
Arthur G. Penny was himself a sort of Sunday poet, a
few other literary books came from the press, including, much later, Penny's own memoirs, *The Shirt-Sleeved
Generation* (1953). The Eagle Publishing Company,
which had been founded as long ago as 1921, was still
active on a small scale as publisher of the Yiddish daily,
the *Kanader Adler,* and the *Canadian Jewish Chronicle* with
which the poet A.M. Klein was long associated.

In 1940 there was certainly a flourishing English book
trade in Quebec. In the Lovell directory for Montreal
for that year there are sixty-nine names listed under
"Publishers" in the classified business directory section.
But of those sixty-nine, which include familiar names
like the Gazette Printing Co., John Lovell & Son Ltd.,
and others, none was issuing trade books (fiction, poetry, belles-lettres, history etc.) on a regular basis. Such
Canadian publishers as were doing so were all in Toronto.
In the *University of Toronto Quarterly* in 1938, Morley
Callaghan described Canada as "a country that is no
publisher's paradise." The truth of his remark applied
then with extra force to Quebec, with its predominantly
French-speaking population. Much later, poet David

McFadden observed that "being an English-speaking poet in Montreal is somewhat akin to being a Ukranian-speaking poet in Windsor or perhaps a Spanish-speaking poet in North Bay."

This was the case in spite of the fact that English Montreal was an important literary centre and had been since the 1920s. Leslie Gordon Barnard and Frank L. Packard, two of the first Canadian writers to live by their work, both resided in Montreal, although they published their books elsewhere. In the middle of the decade, a group of students at McGill University founded the *McGill Fortnightly Review*, a student writing magazine of more than usual interest. In its pages, poets and critics like F.R. Scott, A.M. Klein, Leo Kennedy, Leon Edel, and others took their writerly baby steps and in the process helped to bring Modernism to Canada.

In the 1940s, poetry groups were behind two other magazines of significance, *First Statement* and *Preview*, which later merged to form *Northern Review*. John Sutherland was a poet and critic from the Maritimes who went to Montreal to attend McGill University. He quit after a single term and began *First Statement*, out of which grew a small literary publishing house. First State-

Cerberus

LOUIS DUDEK IRVING LAYTON RAYMOND SOUSTER

Cerberus was the first book published by Contact Press (1952). The cover design of this collection of poems by the three founding editors of the press was by Betty Sutherland, Irving Layton's wife and a well-known Montreal painter in the 1950s.

Pierre Laporte's study of Maurice Duplessis (1960) was
the first book published by Harvest House.

ment Press published only eight books between 1945 and 1951. The printing press and type were sold in the fall of 1950, the last two books being printed for Sutherland by a printer in Vaudreuil, outside Montreal. First Statement Press was therefore a typical small-scale literary press, printing books of poetry by little-known poets in small editions. But because its short list did include Irving Layton, Miriam Waddington, and Raymond Souster, poets who later established serious reputations, the press is of some note. Its office was in a building on Craig Street West, a street which Stephen Leacock described only a few years before the press was founded as "long a blot on Montreal, filled... with the refuse thrown into it."

Sutherland's activities as a magazine and book publisher were the model for a later small publishing house along similar lines. Contact Press was founded in 1952 by poets Louis Dudek, Irving Layton, and Raymond Souster, the first two from Montreal and the third from Toronto. The press grew out of *Contact*, a literary magazine (1952-54), and over the sixteen years it was active would publish some of Canada's best-known poets: Margaret Atwood, George Bowering, Al Purdy, and the three editors themselves. At the time the larger

Toronto-based publishers were mostly uninterested in poetry, and it was Contact Press which really kept alive a literary culture in the 1950s, and prepared the ground for the remarkable flowering of Canadian literature in the 1960s. The editorial and production activities of Contact Press took place predominantly in Montreal in the first few years; but when Layton resigned and was replaced by Peter Miller at the end of the 1950s, most of the press's work shifted to Toronto, although Dudek in Montreal remained as active as ever.

Other new English publishing companies slowly emerged in post-war Montreal, now to all intents and purposes the only centre for English-language publishing in the province. The *Reader's Digest*, which had been founded in 1922, opened a Montreal office in 1948 and a decade later was producing Canadian editions of the magazine in both English and French to a combined total of over a million copies a month. Harvest House, a publishing company owned by Maynard and Ann S. Gertler and still active today, emerged in 1960 with Pierre Laporte's *The True Face of Duplessis*, an ominous first choice at the beginning of that troubled and exciting decade in Quebec. The house has never issued more than a few books a year and specializes in non-fiction, including history, biography, and science. Its "French Writers of Canada" series has included over the years English translations of novels by Yves Thériault, Anne Hébert, Jacques Ferron, and Victor-Levy Beaulieu, among others, as well as the poet Fred Cogswell's translations of the complete poems of Émile Nelligan (1983) and of *The Poetry of Modern Quebec* (1976). Although never much interested in literary publishing (except for translation), Harvest House is certainly in the tradition that includes Louis Carrier (whom Gertler consulted before setting up the company), First Statement Press, and Contact Press: houses that are operated by a small staff and devoted more to a cultural vision than to any potential financial rewards.

About the same time that Harvest House was founded, a committee at McGill University recommended to Principal Cyril James that a university press be founded. On the first of July, 1960, McGill University Press "opened its doors for business ... with a telephone (connected, thankfully) and four bare walls," as Robin Farr, its first director, wrote in the McGill alumni magazine. Farr had worked for Copp Clark in Toronto before moving to Montreal to direct only the second university press in Canada (the University of

Robin Strachan (left) and Robin M. Farr, respectively the
second and first directors of McGill-Queen's University Press,
in 1967. (Reproduced from *The McGill News*.)

Toronto Press being the first). Among the earliest books of the press were a medical book and Morris Bishop's *White Men Came to the St. Lawrence*, the published version of the third Beatty Memorial Lecture series. By 1967, when Farr left and was replaced by Robin Strachan (from Macmillan of Canada), McGill University Press had published some fifty books and was well established as an important academic press. The following year it established a link with Queen's University in Kingston, Ontario, and became McGill-Queen's University Press, the name the press still bears. Today under its current director, Philip Cercone, it publishes around seventy books a year on a wide variety of scholarly and occasionally popular topics.

Literary publishing in English Canada as a whole began to increase in the 1960s. Coach House Press, founded in Toronto in 1965, can be viewed as following in the line of Contact Press, and Raymond Souster certainly felt that because of it there was less of a need to continue Contact Press as the 1960s wore on. In Montreal, Louis Dudek's interest in the press was also waning and his thoughts turned to the founding of a local literary press, Delta Canada, which he established in 1965 with poets Michael Gnarowski and Glen Siebrasse. (Dudek had earlier published poetry books under the imprint of the McGill Poetry Series, including Leonard Cohen's first collection, *Let Us Compare Mythologies*). The press took its name from *Delta*, the literary magazine edited and published by Dudek from 1957-66. The three editors used to meet on Saturday afternoons to do the press's business, as all of them had full-time jobs in the long and noble tradition of small-press publishers. Ron Everson's *Wrestle With an Angel* (1965) was Delta Canada's first book, and some forty others were issued over the years 1965-71, most notably Everson's *Selected Poems* (1970) and Dudek's *Atlantis* (1967) and *Collected Poetry* (1971). When the press was dissolved in 1971, each of the three editors started his own individual one. Siebrasse for a short time published under the name Delta Can in the Montreal suburb of Lasalle, and then joined with the poets Michael Harris and Richard Sommer to issue books under the New Delta imprint (1976-77). Michael Gnarowski, after moving to Ottawa to teach at Carleton University, began the Golden Dog Press. With his wife Aileen Collins, Dudek established DC Books (the initials suggesting its parent, Delta Canada, as well as Dudek/Collins and, as Dudek once remarked, "direct current"), and continued to publish

7 4

Selected
Poems
1920/1970

by R.G. Everson

drawings by Colin Haworth

published by Delta Canada △

The front cover of a Delta Canada book.
Colin Haworth is a Montreal artist who illustrated most
of Ron Everson's books.

The cover of *The Hockey Sweater* (1984), one of
Tundra Books' highly successful children's titles.

poetry mainly by English Quebec poets, among them Laurence Hutchman, Marc Plourde, Henry Beissel, and Avi Boxer. DC Books was sold in 1986 to writer Steve Luxton for a symbolic dollar, and now issues two to four books a year, including fiction and poetry by writers like Dudek (who remains a consulting editor), Robert Allen, Grant Loewen and others, and the regularly published *Moosehead Anthology*.

Cઠ

With DC Books and McGill-Queen's University Press we come to the group of English publishers founded since 1960, which is still in business. (Eden Press, publisher of the highly successful *Anglo Guide to Survival in Québec*, and Optimum Publishing, which evolved out of the publishing activities of the Montreal *Star*, flourished for awhile in the 1980s.) The oldest, May Cutler's Tundra Books, was established in 1967 and was the first Canadian publisher to specialize in children's books. Cutler has been notably outspoken and colourful in a trade known for its outspoken and colourful figures.

At the monthly lunches of the Montreal Publishers Roundtable that led eventually to the founding of the

Association of English-Language Publishers of Quebec (L'Association des éditeurs anglophones du Québec, or AEAQ), Cutler and Maynard Gertler used to invite arts council officials, editors, writers, and media people to talk and to listen, in an attempt to increase the profile of English publishing in Quebec. (Cutler and Gertler did not join the AEAQ when it was first formed, but Cutler later changed her mind and became a member).

Cutler has quarrelled publicly with The Writers Union of Canada and The Canada Council, and her political instincts eventually led to a stint as mayor of Westmount. Tundra has won numerous awards for its books, several of which have become Canadian classics (*Mary of Mile 18* by Ann Blades and William Kurelek's *A Prairie Boy's Winter,* for example), and its list includes well-known writers like Roch Carrier, Stéphane Poulin, Sheldon Cohen and others. Like John Lovell a century before her, Cutler established an American office in 1971 a few miles south of Montreal at Plattsburgh, New York, to take better advantage of the huge U.S. market. For a time she also ran a bookstore in Old Montreal that sold only Canadian books, much like the better known and still active Double Hook in Westmount.

Literary, and in particular poetic, activity in Montreal

grew quite lively in the 1970s, and a good deal of publishing ensued, much but not all of it of a limited or private kind. Most important was the founding of Véhicule Press, which is today a notable Montreal trade publisher. The press took its name from Véhicule Art Inc., a parallel or artist-run gallery founded in 1972 and located at 61 Ste-Catherine West. Within a year, a printing press had been installed in the gallery and poetry books began to appear with the Véhicule imprint. A reading series was also established that year, and eventually a group of seven writers coalesced as the Vehicule Poets (the accent was dropped by the group but maintained by the press), many of whose books were published by the press in the 1970s. Simon Dardick and Guy Lavoie, both founding members of the press, worked with an editorial board from 1976-81 that consisted of three of the poets: Ken Norris, Endre Farkas, and Artie Gold. Dardick, not himself a writer, eventually took over the press in 1981 with his wife Nancy Marrelli. Since then they have turned it into a diversified trade publisher with special interests in Montreal, jazz, the history of science, and fiction. From 1982, Véhicule's poetry list has appeared under a separate imprint, Signal Editions, and is edited by

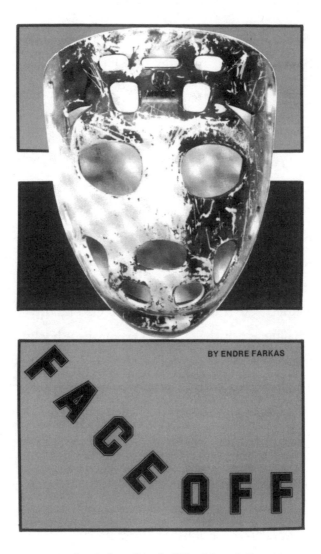

BY ENDRE FARKAS

FACE OFF

Poet Endre Farkas founded The Muses' Company
in 1980. *Face Off,* a book designed like hockey cards,
was its first publication.

Michael Harris.

With the passing of Véhicule Press out of the hands of the Vehicule Poets, the group broke up and moved in different directions. One member, John McAuley, began the short-lived Maker Press, whose imprint is on the poets' group anthology, *The Vehicule Poets* (1979, and printed, perhaps confusingly, at the Véhicule Press).

Endre Farkas started a literary press called The Muses' Company in 1980. The Muses' Company has published about thirty books, beginning with Farkas's *Face Off,* a book in broadside form. The press has published mostly Montreal poets, including many first books, and several from outside the mainstream. One of its books, Kenneth Radu's *The Cost of Living,* was nominated for the 1988 Governor General's Award in the fiction category. Like most writer-run presses, The Muses' Company encourages its writers to be actively involved at all stages in the publishing of their books.

Other small literary presses active in the 1970s included Ingluvin Publications (K. V. Hertz and Seymour Mayne), DaVinci Press (Allan Bealy), Bonsecours Editions (G.C. Ian Burgess), CrossCountry Press (Ken Norris, Jim Mele, and Robert Galvin), and Villeneuve (Fred Louder and Robyn Sarah). Fred Louder was also active as a letterpress printer.

Another literary press born in the 1970s is Guernica Editions, founded in 1979 by Antonio D'Alfonso, a poet and translator. Guernica has been devoted, above all, to bringing out French, English, and particularly Italian writers in both official languages. European and North American writers of Italian origin on its list include Marco Fraticelli, Pasquale Verdicchio, Mary-Jo Bona, and Gianna Patriarcha. Contemporary Quebec poets like Nicole Brossard, André Roy, Yolande Villemaire, France Théoret, Yves Préfontaine, and others have been made available to English readers in translations issued by Guernica. In less than fifteen years D'Alfonso has published over a hundred books, most of them in a small duodecimo size, and his list has included English-language writers like Ken Norris, Dorothy Livesay, and Raymond Filip. Guernica Editions has recently announced plans to move to Toronto.

A few final presses round out the current English publishing scene in Montreal. Karen Haughian's NuAge Editions began life in 1986 as a project in a course given by poet Gary Geddes at Concordia University on publishing and editing. Three of the sixteen students— Odette Dubé and Susan Usher, as well as Haughian—

eventually published four books independently of the university in the late summer of 1987. Dubé and Usher later left the press, which is now run solely by Haughian and has published thirty-two books to date, with some emphasis on fiction, translation, and drama. Among successful NuAge titles have been several plays by Vittorio Rossi and *Birds of Passage*, a first novel by Linda Leith, the editor of *Matrix* magazine. Two NuAge titles have been finalists for the Governor General's awards.

Black Rose Books, coordinated by Dimitrios Roussopoulos and now almost twenty-five years old, publishes books on political and social issues with a radical analysis. Claire Culhane, George Woodcock, and Noam Chomsky have been on the Black Rose list, as well as other important anarchist, ecologist, and feminist writers. Roussopoulos has long been associated with *Our Generation*, an important journal which began in 1961 as *Our Generation Against Nuclear War*, and like May Cutler he has been involved in local politics, having co-founded in 1990 the Ecology Montreal party. The house now publishes roughly twenty books a year, and among its titles is editor Mark Achbar's *Manufacturing Consent: Noam Chomsky and the Media*, based on the successful Canadian documentary film of the same title. Black Rose has recently begun publishing books in French under the separate, but associated imprint Editions Écosociété. Since February of 1993, Écosociété has been publishing original titles on characteristic Black Rose subjects (urban issues, ecology, etc.) as well as French translations of books from the Black Rose list.

Empyreal Press is a small literary house run by Sonja Skarstedt and Geof Isherwood, who once edited a little magazine called *Zymergy*. Shoreline of Ste-Anne-de-Bellevue and Carraig Books of Ste-Foy are two further small presses, the latter specializing in books of Irish interest.

Robert Davies, the son of legendary antiquarian bookseller Raymond Arthur Davies, began his publishing career by issuing facsimiles of Canadiana as Rééditions Québec, and in 1972 founded L'Étincelle, a French-language publishing company. Twenty years later he started Robert Davies Publishing to issue books in English, and his first publication was Pierre Trudeau's so-called Maison Eggroll speech. He afterwards attracted a lot of publicity by bringing out the English translation of Esther Delisle's *The Traitor and the Jew* in 1993, a controversial study of Lionel Groulx. (L'Étincelle had published the French edition in 1992). A recent title from Robert Davies Publishing is an English translation of Jean-Paul de Lagrave's biographical and cultural study of Fleury Mesplet, Montreal's first printer, a book which might appropriately bring this survey to a close.

℘

During most of its 200-year history, English publishing in Quebec has had to survive under special conditions. In its earliest days and in its most recent efflorescence, government patronage has meant survival. In the eighteenth and early nineteenth centuries, a commission to do government printing or the luck to be publishing a newspaper ideologically favourable to the party in power allowed a printer/publisher the financial security occassionally to take on other, more risky projects. Today, The Canada Council, the Canadian Federation for the Humanities, and other governmental agencies, both federal and provincial, make it possible to publish books whose projected sales alone would not justify financially a decision to publish. These conditions applied and apply pretty much uniformly across Canada. Recent discussions between the English writing and publishing community in Quebec and the Minister of Culture and

Communications indicate that government support will increase in the future with anglophone representation on the recently created Quebec Arts Council (Le Conseil des arts et des lettres), and other promising initiatives regarding English culture in the province.

The mid- to late nineteenth century was the heyday of English publishing in Quebec. Increasing literacy resulting from better education, and the absence of competition from radio, television, or the other forms of entertainment that would arrive in the next century, meant that readership was arguably larger on a proportional basis that it had ever been or would ever be again. A massively productive publisher like John Lovell could not have existed in Montreal a century earlier, and certainly could not exist today.

All the same, Montreal was a strongly English-speaking island in a predominantly French-speaking province, and it is not surprising that the shift of publishing power to Ontario that took place at the end of the nineteenth century should have occurred. Canadian publishing began to be dominated by branch offices of foreign publishers, and Toronto must have seemed a more logical base of operations than Montreal in the pre-war years. Most of the new indigenous publishing companies that also sprang up then were founded by men who had trained at the Ryerson Press (as it was called after 1920), and they predictably also chose Toronto as their centre. And so Montreal began to decline steadily as a publishing centre for English books. Louis Carrier revived it briefly in the 1920s, and thereafter there was relatively little activity until the present group came into being over the last thirty or so years. They work under sometimes awkward political conditions, though possibly no more awkward than those under which Fleury Mesplet, for example, worked. Their successes, however, suggest that English publishing in Quebec certainly has a bright future.

A Note on Sources

The main primary source used in the preparation of this study has been the books themselves, some of which I have quoted from or referred to specifically. Any history of publishing must naturally begin with them. The city directories have been highly useful for statistical and other information, and the *Dictionary of Canadian Biography* provided much essential biographical data on a number of the earlier publishers.

The literature on printing and publishing in Canada is still rather thin, but H. Pearson Gundy's *Early Printers and Printing in the Canadas* (Toronto: Bibliographical Society of Canada, 1964) and especially George Parker's *The Beginnings of the Book Trade in Canada* (Toronto: University of Toronto Press, 1985) were helpful. Marie Tremaine's *A Bibliography of Canadian Imprints 1751-1800* (Toronto: University of Toronto Press, 1952) remains the most important study of eighteenth-century Canadian printing.

More specific pieces of the story were found in other sources. Information on Brissot de Warville comes from Robert Darnton's essay "A Spy in Grub Street," in his *The Literary Underground of the Old Regime* (Cambridge and London: Harvard University Press, 1982), pp. 41-70. The 1800 Neilson catalogue is reproduced in facsimile in Sandra Alston, "Canada's First Bookseller's Catalogue," *Papers of the*

Bibliographical Society of Canada 30, 1 (Spring 1992), pp. 4-26. The Caxton anniversary party is described in Richard Virr, "Behold This Treasury of Glorious Things: The Montreal Caxton Exhibition of 1877," *Papers of the Bibliographical Society of Canada* 30, 2 (Fall 1992), pp. 7-20. The Mark Twain story is recounted in Edgar Andrew Collard, *Montreal Yesterdays* (Toronto: Longmans Canada, 1963), pp. 282-88. The George Iles copy of *Huckleberry Finn* is now at McGill. The Watson Griffin letter is in W.D. Lighthall's papers, also at McGill. David Legate recounts his Carrier experiences in his autobiography, *Fair Dinkum* (Toronto: Doubleday Canada, 1969). The Morley Callaghan quote is from "The Plight of Canadian Fiction," *University of Toronto Quarterly* 7, 2 (1938), pp. 152-61, and the David McFadden quote from a review called "A Montreal Anthology," *CVII* 3, 3 (January 1978), pp. 43-44. Stephen Leacock's description of Craig Street is in *Montreal, Seaport and City* (Garden City: Doubleday, Doran, 1942), p. 286. Information on *Reader's Digest* in Canada may be found in James Playsted Wood's *Of Lasting Interest: The Story of the Reader's Digest* (Garden City: Doubleday, 1958). My edition of *The Letters of John Sutherland, 1942-1956* (Toronto: ECW Press, 1992) contains much on First Statement Press and the magazines associated with it, and Michael Gnarowski's *Contact Press, 1952-1967: A Note on Its Origins and a Check List of Titles* (Montreal: Delta Canada, 1970) documents this important small press. The article on the founding of McGill-Queen's University Press referred to is "McGill's Publishing Arm," *The McGill News* 42, 1 (Winter 1960), pp. 23-25.

Information on some of the current Quebec publishers came from telephone interviews and conversations with a a number of people. My thanks to the following: Philip Cercone, May Cutler, Antonio D'Alfonso, Simon Dardick, Louis Dudek, Robert Davies, Endre Farkas, Maynard Gertler, Karen Haughian, Ken Norris, and Dimitrios Roussopoulos.

Index

94

95

96

OTHER TITLES OF INTEREST FROM VÉHICULE PRESS

Raging Like A Fire: A Celebration of Irving Layton. Edited
   by Henry Beissel and Joy Bennett
CIV/n: A Literary Magazine of the 50s. Edited by Aileen
   Collins
*A Man of Sentiment: The Memoirs of Philippe-Joseph Aubert
   de Gaspé 1786-1871*. Translated by Jane Brierley
Yellow-Wolf & Other Tales of the Saint Lawrence. Philippe-
   Joseph Aubert de Gaspé. Translated by Jane Brierley
*Grassroots, Greystones & Glass Towers: Montreal Urban
   Issues and Architecture*. Edited by Bryan Demchinsky
Stone Voices: Wartime Writings of Japanese Canadian Issei.
   Edited by Keibo Oiwa. Foreword by Joy Kogawa
Montreal Photo Album: Photographs from Montreal Archives.
   Edited by Nancy Marrelli
The Writers of Montreal. Elaine Kalman Naves
*The Passionate Debate: The Social and Political Ideas of
   Quebec Nationalism 1920-1945*. Michael Oliver
An Everyday Miracle: Yiddish Culture in Montreal. Edited
   by Ira Robinson, Pierre Anctil, and Mervin Butovsky

Distributed by General Distribution Services.